T0193565

Poetically
Unique

Poetically Unique

John Petrosius

POETICALLY UNIQUE

Copyright © 2017 John Petrosius.

All rights reserved. No part of this book may be used or reproduced by any means, graphic, electronic, or mechanical, including photocopying, recording, taping or by any information storage retrieval system without the written permission of the author except in the case of brief quotations embodied in critical articles and reviews.

iUniverse books may be ordered through booksellers or by contacting:

iUniverse
1663 Liberty Drive
Bloomington, IN 47403
www.iuniverse.com
1-800-Authors (1-800-288-4677)

Because of the dynamic nature of the Internet, any web addresses or links contained in this book may have changed since publication and may no longer be valid. The views expressed in this work are solely those of the author and do not necessarily reflect the views of the publisher, and the publisher hereby disclaims any responsibility for them.

Any people depicted in stock imagery provided by Thinkstock are models, and such images are being used for illustrative purposes only. Certain stock imagery © Thinkstock.

ISBN: 978-1-5320-3366-7 (sc)
ISBN: 978-1-5320-3367-4 (e)

Library of Congress Control Number: 2017915046

Print information available on the last page.

iUniverse rev. date: 09/30/2017

Contents

Trying hard to let go

The more I try the worst it seems
I'd have a happy home if I let it be
I explain myself but got nothing to show
I'm like a suction cup it's hard to let go

"How long do you think it's going to last?"
It's a stupid question—I know, I go too fast
My head's in my hands dumb as it sounds
I'm on the floor in mental pain rolling around

I push you to your limits of letting it be
The tiger's mouth is open giving details of me
I know my limits and try to explain
My problems are irritating and a little insane

Being me is hard so don't bring me down
I imagine something better than hanging around
I bang heads with "what" then I sing the blues
But leaving it alone just isn't what I do

A Different View

Other people besides me
Live here in this world
It's all about perspectives
What view do you see?

Say I'm nine and I want candy
Mommy won't give it so she's my enemy
Somedays she comes home from working late
When her friends are with her I got to wait

When that happens she hardly even says "Hi"
"It smells good—what's cooking?" says I
"It's not for you, get upstairs and play."
She made me cry—I want her to die

The ashes from that thing in her mouth
Dropped on my nose, she slaps me and points
"Come down when the guest are done!"
Upstairs I play with my cars, matches and guns

Time is like a train

Time is like a speeding jet train,
And I'm like the little kid inside
Looking out the window pane
My tongue going side to side

I watched my childhood passed by
Scanned grey, new mornings that won't last
Watching the smoke from the chimneys rise
They look like little tornados as we pass by

I kept checking my watch
And wondering if this train
Is going to stop and leave its
Passengers at their destination

But, by the time the train did stop
I needed help to get me out
My hair was white and my back bent
My speeding jet train was heaven sent

Whisperings

You're whispering images I obey
You can't disrupt my heart anymore anyways
I live companionless on your highway—while my
Thoughts are occupied with your dark-light night and day

I wake up to your whispers
As they swirl in my mind
Hissing out your secrets
About my friends to leave behind

Your vile breath haunts the inside my skull
Putrid images that you use helps the hatred grow
Until I push the warm snuggling memories away
And trust your true-lie secrets day to day

There is no use running or escaping from you
You already changed me that's what you do
You entered into my atmosphere that's clear
Now I'm clothed in your suspicions and fear

The pain of living

You don't even care
If I really hurt
You make your plans
Like everyone on earth

You say you're open
But you're really closed
I give you my life
Yet you turn up your nose

We had our talks that
Lasted way into the night
We came to conclusions
That some things aren't right

But we said what we wanted
And now we'll leave it alone
It's just unfinished business—
Not our final gravestone

Who are you afraid of?

Knocking at your door
You know who I am
I'm your friend, we just talked
Are you going to let me in?

You're peeking around your curtains
And you haven't got much on
You know why I'm out here—so
Stop being crazy and let's get it on

Your love messages are on my table
From your phone calls to my home
But that's when you were hot and able
I guess your love is only for the phone

So … who are you afraid of?
It's not this thing called "love"
So let me in—you arranged this
At least, reach out and give me a hug

Leaving the Past

It's hard to let it be
Or leave it alone
When I'm being ignored
Or when you're never at home

It's not working! This isn't fastball!
It's hard to not react to a disappearing
Relationship that's gone AWOL
I miss it and want it back—that's all

You're sitting alone
Listening to your thoughts,
Playing one of those mindless app game
Being as careless as Goldilocks in her home

I find I have vanished into my life too
I can't believe what's happening to me and you
We want our freedom more than each other
It might not be right but … it's true I shudder

Time

Time is rugged like a mountain
We climb it, our hands bleeds,
It's hard to tell how long it takes us
We triumph the peak and from it see

The clouds resemble a lake below us
The mountain range goes on for miles
The weather blows with blistery gusts
My bones ache, not only me but all of us

After a minute we slide down the other side
Our struggles were bitter we hardly got hide
Pretty much everything looks the same to me
Ferns pass by swiftly from inside this tapestry

"Tomorrow we'll be there," someone roars
But when we tried to stand we were stiff as boards
A white haired woman whispers, "Grab a stick
I think we're too exhausted to talk anymore."

The Mental paths of anger

I'm angry because you
Are controlling my life
And I don't make a choice
Unless you give me your—nod

I feel you and
Your approvals now
If I say anything
I'm starting a fight—what's the odds

I'm slow,
I let things go,
I drop things
And I don't bring it up—so

When I compare my life
With anybody else's
I want to kick off my shoes
And start walking down—the highway

Hiding out inside my house

Bringing up the past, things we used to do
People we knew, who are still cooking in our stew
It's like doing hard time, we got to let it go
It's the same old, same old ... same old show

I go in my house, sit and do my thing
With heartstrings, upswings and ding-a-lings
Or maybe it's the selfish way they're reasoning
Talking right through me like a plaything

Why do I even hang out with this obsolete mob?
Where is it going? Every one of them are slobs?
So I'm leaving and staying indoors to hibernate,
That's where I'll trim my thought trees in peace

The unexpected and funny thing I find out later is ...
I wasn't missed at all—I didn't drop the ball
So hiding in my house without them was a good thing
I got it right and learned a lesson so isn't this a happy ending

Do I hear voices or what?

Them creeping little logics
That comes with reasons
You know what I mean?
"Do it now or lose the opportunity"

Or "Are you sure you're not going
To need it later?" says the voice.
It gives you the reasons and then
Gives you another very logical choice

You do know this "voice" isn't you
But—what can you say
It's got to be true—Right?
Because it wasn't me so who's "the who"?

Creepy crossroads in our lives
Suggesting voices are turning us
Little harmless looking things
Veering us off like children

The wrong side of my bed

You know that feeling like you
Got out of the wrong side of the bed
Well that's the feeling I got today
Like someone's sitting on my head

Whatever I say or do
I feel criminalized or demonized
Or like I'm always apologizing
For being me to you

Why do I even bother to get up?
Is it a bad habit or just a bad lust?
My blankets got me all wrapped up
I need coffee but just broke my cup

It's the wrong side of the bed syndrome
The Doc told me that in a dream
Like being in some poor Devil's scheme
I'm in a fog—I'm living but not seen

Soap

Is there any strong soap
To use to wash all—I hope
All my stupid living patterns
The ones I didn't think mattered—down the sink

Why re-invent myself
I can't cover up all these stains
I might try to bleach it out
But nothing will take away the blame

These cosmetics that are around
Do work wonder if you're a clown
But nothing can take away my
Sadness and these real frowns

But these stains that I have
They go way too deep for me
I need someone who cares and
To clean everything that's dirty

Life: Here we go again

I feel like: I'm going down a tunnel
But the only tunnels I gone through
Were a sewer, or the kind in parks
Or Alabama's Mobile Bay, that was cool

I feel like: telling everyone I know …
But why would I tell them anything
Since they are the ones who don't listen
And I don't think they were ever my friends

I feel like: I don't want to be with anyone,
I just want to be with my thoughts all alone
Maybe going to the shoreline for a walk
Or checking on rentals for a new home

I feel like: jumping on a slow freight,
Or taking my little boat out with me
Moving along in the breeze or breaking
My phone and not listening to them again

This old damn road

You're watching me so close
What are you looking for?
I see you—but who
Is looking back at me?

Why ask these question?
Don't you really know?
I am going through struggles—
Help me or leave me alone?

I feel like you want to find something—
Are you really going to look? Tear it up,
Dig it up, burn it up or throw it up
Really it's going to be that hard? But why?

I hide things, don't you know?—
I do it because I fear being told.
"So tell me—why do we always
Have to go down this *old damn road*?"

The Singer

Finding fault isn't hard to do
Hair hanging as he steps into the room
To him nothing seems to matter
Then he strikes his first chord

The music is simple, two chords or three
His young smooth voice starts slowly
The words dart into their heart's lighted tunnels
Into doors within hiding so refined and subtle

He sings his songs off hand written paper
From a table placed before him by the host
Who is un-expectantly mystified by the singer
As she watches his small audience tears well up

The words of his songs awakens the few who hears
Melodies as an elixir that gives hope with anti-fear
His words has a mixture of logic and absurdities
Not even a cough as the room goes quiet magically

Slave days

Finish it—do it, plan it—
Complete it—show it—
Paint it—eat it
And now come get it

Life goes on
As it spins in orbit
With a bunch of *I got to do this*
And *I got to do that's.*

Pride and
False humility
Is right behind us
On their sterling silver horses

No pain in the chasing of lust
Only in the losing that quest
That quest gets hard to perform
To perform another slave day

Just talking about it

My mind's on the blink
My stomach's down the sink
Too much of that brownie I ate
And it sure wasn't chocolate cake

"This was my last cigarette!"
Habits like this get me to regret
The first time they were cool
But now there's just too many rules

I'm tired of not being complete
Needing that "something" to make me "me"
I was born in this world wasn't that enough?
Do I have to go on proving I can get more stuff?

These inner, crying, gnawing, clawing needs
Are opening my eyes to what's inside of me
When it comes to contentment and being free
It appears to me we're all just "wanna-bees"

Cuteness

They hide behind their cuteness
Curly cues, and false meekness
Obscure their own weakness
You can't fight their right-ness

Cute animals in the stores
Old men bend to itch them
Grabs attention galore
Woman poop-scoops them

Look! Adorable collars
Prancing and smiling
Can you hear the begging?
As real humans' holler?

We're warped these days
In our unequal ways—and
As for the love of animals
Who cares anyways?

What's wrong with being me?

I hear that I should be
All the things I want to be.
But what is the motive or what lies
Behind that question—let's see

Why is it that I can't just be me?
Do I have to choose my life externally?
This place is so hard and cruel
It's ridiculous to learn all their rules

What's wrong with being where I'm at?
Growing in my heart yet never learning too fast
When I'm done with my education of letting it be
I'll drop the dross and see what's left in me

What's wrong—I like to know
With moseying down the street
Talking to myself, making up new songs
Walking really slow—down any road

Not knowing who you are

Not knowing who you are
I didn't ask you the question
But turned my head and winked
And grinned in another direction

The white snow drifted abundantly—as
I gazed at a cyclone fence behind me
A fence only a dust devil will see—and
If a cyclone came that would amaze me

The dry wind and the cactuses
Clouds of dust and killer bees
One tornado can make messes
Against my senses it would be

But if we ever did get a cyclone—I'm
Sure it will be like Dorothy's and Toto's
So, here's the question now that we're acquainted
Why have a cyclone fence if you live in the desert?

Love is in the air

You hold my heart with your hands
Both of them wrapped gently around it,
Time stands still, light penetrates,
Layers of callous crumbles to the ground

It is possible that once it's made alive
That it can forever be satisfied
Something I thought I had to do
But I see my heart and believe it's new

It's like a yawn, a new cut lawn, a new year,
Slipping it into a brand new gear, going somewhere
A peaceful song, doing nothing wrong
And shooting a squirt gun in the face of my friend

I like seeing a smiling child, clothes on a line
And flapping drying shirts being blown on a wintery day,
Holding hands, talking to understand, and drinking coffee
Then a milkshake from the same straw—love is in the air

The power of understanding

If only lies
Can calm your heart.
Then what will truth
Bring you?

If you say love.
Then I'd say "Oh really?"
Why? Because I understand
What you are going through.

I wish I could help you
And say and give you more
But you need what I can't give
And that's your own experiences

So be of good cheer don't worry about a thing
Because Jesus Christ became our name and king
He overcame this prison by paying for our crimes
The truth is simple do you think you can believe this time?

On the spiritual side

The hum of a swarm of bees
Seductive winds being blown
Swimming circles faster to see
Dizzy youth in a group alone

Cars and free time
And smiles and flirts
Sunshine and beginnings
And young guy in flappy shirts

Fine wines and cool cars
And manners galore
Living for laughter and
Drinking and doing more

When the wine is drunk
And you're on your knees
Gone are the friends
Aloneness is all you'll see

An Act of Love

"Will you please close the door?"
She asked kindly and with a sweet grin
Undercurrents blasted but she didn't give in
"I hope you understand my little man?" Patting his chin

"You'll get your turn later—I'm sure of it, wait in line."
But, I want mine now!" the red faced, little boy whined
She turned and squeezed her doll "I got something else
I got to do," and passed it to the boy. "Would you?"

The door went "slam" as a gust went through
The boy stood on the porch and started to stew
The wind was blowing paper, sticks and leaves
Trees were being blown down it was a scary scene

"Do it yourself," he screamed.
Just then a gust of wind pick him up
And blew him down the street—
Screaming and crashing into a truck

But ... can you listen?

It hurts being me,
Stomaching the simple
When they don't take
What I say seriously

I see it clearly,
Think about it daily
And say it, but they don't
Believe any of it.

"Knuckleheads!" I say to myself
As I stamp around my room
Promising myself that I won't
Say another word to these fools

But eventually, my silence
Has to be broken, even I
Can't take myself seriously
In the end we all need friends

Just an object for the shelf

"Help me!" you say
But it's only a lure
For you to get
Your own way

And your way
Isn't my way,
But it might appear
Like it is somdays

You cry like a Panda
Or the devil for me,
Calling out, following me,
And looking up from bended knees

But as soon, (zoom, zoom)
As you get the help you need
You'll find something wrong—then
On the shelf (plop) the end of me

Not Holding a Record of Wrong

Who is not holding a record of wrong?
If you see them they're moving on
To the next moment
Like singing a song

Really by doing that
They're letting life go on
Letting free the thread
For the tapestry's song

People are so quick to find faults
Saying words they shouldn't ought
Maybe that is not so wrong
Seems like we like to argue and talk

I guess it doesn't matter
What we think or say
At least we like to think so
So is this love?—that way?

Swimming in the blues

"Swimming in the blues," I said to who.
"You don't care—nobody cares
But Oh!—If this was you?
How the whole world would hear."

I squirm
To make you see
I strive
For your approval of me

I study the people
And watch your response
I attempt to imitate
The smallest nuance

At the cliffs I walk with suicide
We share a bottle and have a few drinks
Together we look down its steep sides
I peruse the landscape—He winks

No Motive to Trace.

"But she can't be that way. Can she?"
Looking for the kill hiding in the bushes
Waiting for the sting
Her claws are out

She's a malicious killing cat
Cutting and licking you up—little morsels
No blood and no apparent motive to trace
No one even thinks that it could be her

She's standing outside the door, waving her curls,
Looking innocent—seeing nothing wrong at all
"It's only a meal and I was hungry—
You can't keep a good cat down"

Her nails are out
Her eyes are darting
She's looking for blood
No motive to trace.

Quiet on discovery

Naturally, I'm concerned about me
If they like me and how I am perceived
Especially now that I am old—because
Before I arrive they want me to go

Now from this new point of view
I have to ask all of you
Why is it when you get old
No one lets you be young?

Just because I'm elderly doesn't
Mean I'm not at least adequate
And even if I did some good
No one sees me and considers it

I'm a little mesmerized
Watching drips of rain
Cascading down a branch
But I'm quiet on my discovery

A Child Within

"I don't belong here," I heard within
The voice that I heard wasn't seen
But I'm not ignoring the fact again
That it could have come from me

I've heard of people, the "weird" ones,
Who listens to voices in their heads
No one wanted anything to do with them
They were afraid they might get dead

But it does kind of make sense
That there are invisibles around us
Some are our prison guards
And others wants to free us

But I did hear a child crying within
And I knew that this child was me
But who is the "me" who lives here
And hopes for its day to be free

2016 Elections

National attention
Forget to mention
You can't figure out
What to say

It has been counted
And can't be erased
If I say anything
You'll get into my face

Whinny
And complaining
Nothing's
Right but you

If education
Is the answer
Why don't you
Go back to school

A Little Angry

I spit my words, I'm red in the face
"To the moon Alice! Kick you into space
Do you know I'm always waiting for you?
You drag your heels putting on your shoes."

Sitting on my porch watching the trains go by
My mind is racing—I don't know why
We got to do what we got to do
But the clock is drooping as I'm waiting for you

When I ask politely are we going to be on time?
You say you'll be ready "Being late ain't no crime!"
I could see right there by the words you say
That for me it's going to be one of these days.

So I get in the car waiting for you dear
The radio's on singing about some beer
I'm tapping my fingers and biting my nails
I swear you're slower than a slimy snail

Help for the Day

The point of view from people
Are cloudy, narrow, and strange
Through sideway glances and tinted glasses
I'm dirty, lazy and probably insane

Old memories pass through their minds
They know who I am—I'm one of the slime
This is my corner, I'm hanging my sign
That's my game—I'm known as "Mister No-Name"

Window barely down, their hand touches air
And drops the wrinkled dollar to the ground
I return their glance as their head turns around
Only to hear the woman in the car behind holler

"I need a meal," my sign reads, "and thirst
For a little water." On the other side it read
"I could work too!—Go ahead and you choose!
If you do it right!—I'll pray for you!"

What else is there to do?

Time erases somethings
Others stay—what the heck
I can stand on the Grand Canyon
And drop a watch with no regrets

Over and over in excuse-land
You explain what happened
"I don't see it your way," I shout
"Shut-up, it smells like you're crapping!"

But the tension reverberates again
I say, "Leave it be or have no friends."
But another comes in and gives it his best
So it starts on over "the wicked has no rest"

To be wrong and yet to be right too?
I heard this before so what else is there to do?
We can bring in the fat and start another chew
Or drop it forever and live by this rule—cool?

The Writer

Those lazy fools broke the rules,
Invented schools, made lies cool
And gave society
New meanings …

He took his "what ifs"
And pen
His paper and jotted down
"The war is won!"

Plenty of warning
From writers
The forgotten past
Believing it will last

There at the bottom he saw it
Screaming and yelling
From the large to small
Looks—from books—telling it all

Rooms

I might just be in a room
Another room of my house,
A house that is inside of me
With many rooms in and out

Rooms forgotten, but when seen
Memories stir and roar back into me
Some rooms fear pushes me away
Other gives feelings that it's not today

If this house is really mine
Why do I sense like I can't even dine?
Also when I talk to others about my rooms
No one admits they have theirs too

But inside our house there's doors
With invisible hanging signs with words
Writings that transcends our mind with script
That says "not worthy to come in yet."

Patients

I'm shocked, all is weird
I got off my mental path
Looking around in double mirrors
Seeing me in a million folds

My thoughts are disorganized
What was right is now left
I'm chasing lust thinking that it is real
Backwards and lost looking for my home

I'm reacting to memory loss,
Confusion and flashing lights
Should I go on? The street has ended
Right here in front of me—I'm alone

Meaningful conversations
Up and down questions
Shouting to rule the roost
Laughing hilariously all afternoon

New Faces

Your face changes
And so does your voice
You're stern and correct sharply
You would never have done that before

You present yourself to me with smiles
Your own particular hocus-pocus
It's phony and unsettling to me
Like a new face I never knew

You correct me as if
You're my third grade teacher
Teaching me your
New right and wrongs

You now talk of Jesus
As if he just opened your eyes
And that I should take notice
But all I see is your new disguise

Doing it now

This is the time to get up
To take a ride and get out
To spend a night or two
With a trusted friend by my side

I'm tested and molested
Suggested and directed
Deluded and eluded
In the hallways of my mind

There's no one that's around me
But their presence I do feel
Their *invisibility* is always working
On changing my beliefs and my will

I get those crazy feelings
And thoughts all the time
Cause without those crazy feelings
They're only pictures in my mind

The Purple Gummy Bear

The gummy bear
Was under the water
Waving his hand upward
Straight in my direction

I picked it up and wiped it dry
And squeezed it and made it cry
I opened my mouth but changed my mind
I knew it was different so ran home to hide

I wanted to eat that purple gummy bear
The kind that did more than tastes like wine
So I put it into my mouth wondering why
And chewed it slowly—now it was inside

It had a little weird taste to it at first—and
It gave me a little kick, otherwise it was fine
I walked over and put my old rock and roll albums on
And then ordered a pizza and ate whatever came to mind

Escaping to be me

I get a thought, an idea,
And I follow it
It takes me to a place
That I shouldn't be

But I say to myself
"I'm only learning,"
And what is happening
Isn't really me.

So I look out the window
And into the street
What is happening is magic
And it's tasting mighty sweet

Where is the hypnotist?
Is she hiding away?
Why am I tinkling?
Who is in my brain anyways?

A Good Visit

"Good-bye, it's been a good visit,
Yes, I'm going back home.
No, I'm not going to travel this month
I'm staying home and going to be alone."

I might not be irritated now
But I know it's coming on
I need my space and get out of the race
Living in two places is an oxymoron

I need my routine
And my places to go
With no kids around
To get my life in the flow

"Thanks for coming around
It was good to see you and your family
After I recoup I'll give you a call, but …
Didn't we have fun stuffing ourselves with candy?"

Waiting for love

Nothing is really
The same with you,
Your eyes don't sparkle
The way they use to do

We walk along
A lonely sidewalk somewhere
You look at your phone
And your heart's not here

I know we had better
But what the heck
Waiting for love
Is a pain in the neck

I know I am the cause
It's like skin from a snake
But I'm trying this time
Is it really that late?

The Friend Club

You have to overlook a lot
To be with friends and family
They expect so much from you
Anticipate them to break the rules

They feel as though they deserve, "We'll
Come be with you for a week or two?"
That wasn't a request, it was a test,
A mess, a conflict, but then what the heck

There is a "choice" but it's hard to see
Either be "friendly" or really be me
I could be agitated and show what I got
Or chose to take a trip around the block

It's like, there's this "family and friends club"
You pay dues daily and you better know the rules
It has been set up "way" before we were born
The expectations are real with limitless scorn

It is starting over again

That look, those looks
These eyes of hatred
And those eyes
Behind the eyes—

What do you think you'll find?
Do you think I'll show where I'm at?
And then, you know me, what about you?
With my tongue I'll dig on you—tit for tat

I shouldn't let this stuff bother me—not really
But I do, especially when you're judging me
I can't be cool with you criticizing my every move
It's hard for me to act naturally—can't you let it be

During the day we might do stuff together and have fun
We talk and laugh and smile and act decent—it's okay
But during this calm, this lull, we watch each other—you know
Then these eyes dart, dig things up, and then the circle starts again.

Finishing the Argument

A little wink, a finger to the brow
A gnawing in the stomach,
And the chewing of the lower lip
Like the cud of a cow

They all talk about it like it was candy
They hand it out all wrapped up nice
Some has more and some has less
But does anything pass their taste test?

It rolls off of their tongues
Like crushed ice, but sweet,
Shimmering like bait fish,
And captivating with heat

Perhaps, because of the winter
Or because the ground is wet
And again, there is nothing happening
So with truth there is nothing to regret

Laughing is a requirement

My face is covered with muck
From years of target practice
Caused by my world's "What the fucks"
As if my expressions can solve anything?

Stuck—choices hanging high
Like a rose tossed at a wedding
Hands lifted, half hoping, eyes riveted
Being animated to catch the bouquet

Fear—that a train could be backing up silently
Towards us with no blinking red lights—scary
Running alongside the railroad tracks
The sound of gravel crackling in my ears

Houses—we should be inside our houses
But the warm dusk and laughter brings us out
Like crickets, the heated nights causes us to sing
And look for the exciting trouble we could get in

Splat

Drums of happiness
Chasing after me,
Especially the Bigger,
Better, and More variety

It's not that any of that stuff
Is more evil than the next
It's how we're wired in our mind
We struggle to get, then struggle with regret

Calculating and fantasying
Warring mentally, fending off the takers
Iron storages and cameras to endeavor to keep it
And I don't have any mind left for precious peace

To catch a thing that catches me
That holds me captive and exhibits me
It's called the "running into a wall" syndrome
But it should be —"the beating of a sin drum"

Making Castles in dreams

Making castles
Out of nothing
Dreams out of wind
And letting them grow

Rock and Roll
Don't you know?
Letting things go
Absolutely no goals

A world unseen
Giving up the seen
Looking pass all the luxury
And the man-made schemes

Hidden magic life, a kind
With laughter and no strife
Content with my children and wife
Working late in t-shirts and jeans

The World will spin

The world will still spin
Even if we don't do a thing
Laying down, looking like a clown
And watching dandelions dance around

Scoping at patterns outside my window
And there's other stuff chiming in
There's something wrong with my day
I can't explain what's not okay

Walking in the rain, looking insane
Saying anything, nothing to explain
Loving til dawn, nothing's ever wrong
Peddling in the mud, getting squeeze hugs

Laying on the lawn
A peaceful long yawn
Nothing to get in my way
Love is more than a word today

Being at Ease

Fairness: It's an easy word,
Easy to understands☹
Everyone kind of knows
What it means

Say you're a new kid,
You're bullied, ☹
Not being told the truth,
And being teased

There is no one
To show you what is normal ☹
And no one to show you
What are the rules

But then someone eventually
Gives you a nudge, ☺
Hands you a drink
And tells you what's cool

The timeless Bob who is the "Bobber"

A break in time, a rest for the mind,
Memories that agitate, I committed no crime
A lonely stretch, no end in sight, a soundless breeze
A little creek, and a shady tree to spend the night

A living stage, not knowing what to say
A timeless bum, being on the run,
Being misunderstood, living as I could,
Laughing until dawn until the never ending yawn

Another ball and chain, and looks from the insane,
Laughter at will, getting over the hill
Holding my head high, trying to be still
Things are taken wrong, especially Butchie's songs

"I don't want life, there's nothing here to gain,
I won't push or strive to live in the fast lane,
I laugh when I'm tickled," the old man said with a grin
He then crossed his legs and shook his head, and then …

Faces from my past

I removed the broken glass
And stones from her hair—
And picked out her ribbons
From the spokes of the motorcycle

Unnatural and unnerving
Do our pale masks come down—?
My eyes were red
And my mind hurt

Boiled cabbage smells fills my lungs
As I stand alone, separated, in my darkness
I move robotically through my precious rubbish
Tearing pieces of her off the bent up expensive metal

I was warned of this day—in a dream or perhaps a da-ja-vu
Funny how we know we knew after things like this happen
But only afterwards can we say that we knew
It's like we were shown, but couldn't apprehend its language

Daily Dilemmas

My daily dilemmas
Wash yesterday's pressures away
New problems are so important
Like bombs or lice either way

The fear of any new hurts
Or horrible problems too
Are combating in my mind
Like snakes, attacking you know who

It gets rough and dirty
Having filth thrown around
Wild thoughts, nervous energy,
And weird groaning sounds

I get drenched with dilemmas
Expectations and me falling apart
They're all mostly mental ones
But some do attack my heart

In the flesh

If there is a place
This weary man can go
I want to be first on the list
To get rest and cast off this load

We live in a world—
Where the flesh matters
We're taught to have a lot of things,
And don't let your mind be scattered

We get shoved around
Pushed into many holes
Made to fix and carry
Then told how to relax

It's a decaying matter, this life
We never get what we started for
We get older, uglier, tired and sore
To do their schemes and a little more

Colorful Lively Dreams

I see your eyes, color blue
Penetrating, spacing out
And looking through me
And not seeing what is true

Life is my pillow I lay my head on
And dream as if in another world
Watching my other life moves on
With my colorful lively dreams

Some nights I'm looking for a
Hole in the side of a mountain
Some paths attached to nothing
Floating high up in a hazy sky

I avoid distractions when awaken
Such as worries, wants and soap
And wait for night fall to come—so
I can sail away in my rainbow boat

Shall we have war?

I guess we need to hate
Something or somebody
Or otherwise I think
We would feel naked

And dark and alone
With no people or things
To put down and find fault with
So we could feel bigger and wiser

Otherwise we might
Turn on ourselves
And find fault and pull
On our loose threads. …

So should we keep on having
Wars and rumors of wars
Just because we don't want
Ourselves to be self-attacked?

Popcorn Nation

Your rules and laws
Do drives me insane
You always have some
Important thing to gain

Why do you exist
In every generation?
You build your bonds
In the heart of every nation

You make us bow down
To all your threats
And then you hand out
Your cigarettes

But they'll come a time
We all hope and suppose
You'll pay for your crimes
And be exposed

Keep slander from yourselves

It's okay for you to say what you say
I'm just doing time—so it's no crime.
So, even if I say bad stuff about you
Even if it's not true—it's cool?

And to find fault with another
I wouldn't want it done to me
So why do I not even bother
To drag a neighbor into the slimy sea

I can't destroy my brother's name
And household and not get a little singed
It might look temporary on the outside
But it stays a long time within

So walk away from it don't let it begin
And slap your hand across your mouth,
Don't listen—don't let the poison in
Do nothing—give it a year to sink in

The Happy Road

Out of the oven
And into the dryer
Spinning around and around
Watching my world expire

Perfect, shady roads, climbing
Through hobbit hills, yes they have them still
The little fires smoking sweet meat
Where the ogres are considering their kill

And the wolves are howling,
Scary things hiding, trees talking
Leaves whooshing, moon shimmering
And little girls walking and trolls stalking

Their giggling's exciting
And their talking's stimulating
To the eyes that are stalking
It's such a happy road to be walking

The old rusty chair

You sit on me,
I hold your weight
You really don't care
I'm just your old rusty chair

Your mind isn't excited—and
There's no memories to explain
You don't cuddle like you use to
It doesn't seem the same

Maybe a can of color
Change me into something new?
Something that can be tolerated
Something yellow or blue

You feel my rust and bumps
But can't I support you
So sand and paint me! ...
The dump just wouldn't do.

Don't you want peace?

Is your peace diseased? Are you
Looking in another direction?
Perhaps, Peace is standing here now?
Waiting for you to do something.

Do you talk about that someone?
That someone who took away your peace?
That somebody who tricked you? Or
That someone who doesn't respect you?

Can you sit still long enough to see your faults?
Remembering your words of that heated conversations?
Or the hard, cutting, hurting words from your mouth?
When you have put their innards on a chopping block?

Is peace worth embracing, even though
You feel that no one is respecting you?
And doesn't remember any of your good
Works or words? … Can you drop it?

Is peace worth embracing? Is it worth a penny?
Or a dime, perhaps a dollar, or two,
Maybe it's not worth much now,
But when you're old—it will be worth more.

An upbeat-ed world

The morning sunshine reminds me
Of my ship wreck in the night
Too many disquieting dreams
My mind's running into blight

Inspiration is covered with the lid of new logic
The a garbage can that ferments and reeks with philosophy
And the questions I would normally answer ... I dodge it
I am closed mouthed because I really don't understand

I'm hopeless
For this hopeful generation
Where it appears that self-confidence
And being cute with warm smiles are their only cure—

I look at my pillow and turn my eyes inward
As I roam through my mental forest with thoughts
Observing images pulsating with electrical cracklings
While watching my felt bugs disturbingly coming nearer

Travel Light and Travel Fast.

Clutter, clutter
The weight of it smothers
A little bit here and entanglement there
Weighed down and going nowhere

Live like, whatever stuff
You do today, no matter how fun.
You won't bring with you
Into tomorrow

We don't need it
But we'll keep it
We're heavier than
An iron snowball on thin ice

So if we can do what we can't do today
We won't let yesterday get in the way
Tomorrow we don't think about at all
Then travel fast and light to Arkansas

Helplessly Hopeful

How can you look at my crimes?
And say that everything is okay?
I struggle to be good
But I get in my way

I'm so use to being slammed down, put down,
Turned around for being so low down.
Then shoved out of the way for doing it my way
And for the fun of it thrown down hard on life's highway

But with you it's not that way
You're the same today, tomorrow,
And the next day—you don't play that game
To you, I'm not a plastic throw away

In fact, it was you who pick me up
Swatted my butt, swept my pants,
Gave me an eye-twinkle smile and another change
As you watched my heals kick up wildly at the dance

Printed in the United States
By Bookmasters